WATERLOO LOCAL SCHOOL
Middle School Library Title II

AUTO RACING

AUTO RACING

CHARLES COOMBS

illustrated with 55 photographs

William Morrow and Company
New York

BY THE SAME AUTHOR
Aerospace Pilot
Aerospace Power, *a Pictorial Guide*
B-70, *Monarch of the Skies*
Bush Flying in Alaska
Cleared for Takeoff, *Behind the Scenes at an Airport*
Deep-Sea World, *the Story of Oceanography*
Drag Racing
Gateway to Space
Lift-Off, *the Story of Rocket Power*
Motorcycling
Project Apollo, *Mission to the Moon*
Project Mercury
Rockets, Missiles, and Moons
Skyhooks, *the Story of Helicopters*
Skyrocketing Into the Unknown
Spacetrack, *Watchdog of the Skies*

Acknowledgments for Photographs
American Motors Company, 8, 45, 67; Ashland Oil, Inc., 5, 25, 26, 82; Bear Manufacturing Company, 51, 68; British Leyland Motors, Inc., 36; Champion Spark Plug Company, 3, 17, 30, 87; Chrysler Motors Corporation, 13, 33, 47; Coombs, Charles, 2, 6, 11, 19, 27, 37, 50, 56, 58, 65, 66, 74, 75, 76, 81, 91, 93; Firestone Tire & Rubber Company, 12, 69, 78; Ford Motor Company, 18, 32, 38, 71; Goodyear Tire & Rubber Company, 40, 63, 85; Infoplan, 43; Ontario Motor Speedway, 7, 49, 54, 61, 80, 88; Reynolds Metals Company, 21, 39; Trackside Photo Enterprises, 83

Copyright © 1971 by Charles Coombs. All rights reserved. No part of this book may be reproduced or utilized in any form or by any means, electronic or mechanical, including photocopying, recording or by any information storage and retrieval system, without permission in writing from the Publisher. Inquiries should be addressed to William Morrow and Company, Inc., 105 Madison Ave., New York, N. Y. 10016. Printed in the United States of America. Library of Congress Catalog Card Number 73-153770
4 5 75 74 73

CONTENTS

Auto Racing   7
The Racing Circuits   15
The Speed Machines   24
Road Courses and Ovals   42
The Drivers   55
The Wrenches   64
The Race   73
Glossary   94
Index   95

The race is on.

AUTO RACING

"Gentlemen, start your engines!"

Shafts spin in their bearings. Exhaust pipes cough awake, and the roar of unmuffled power fills the air. Soon the starter flicks his green flag. Cheers erupt from the excited crowd.

The race is on.

Automobile racing has been with us ever since man invented the piston engine. When he bolted it into the frame of a horseless carriage back in the 1890's, the automobile was born. Undoubtedly two automobiles

Running smoothly.

must have raced on some rutted dirt country road shortly after.

And automobiles have been racing ever since, much to the delight of people around the globe. In fact, next to horse racing, automobile racing in its many forms draws the largest attendance of any sport in the world today.

The popularity seems well earned. Auto racing offers a vast amount of exciting action for both participant and fan. The sleek, high-powered racing machines stimulate the senses of all who work on them, drive them, or simply view the action.

An early road race.

There are many forms of car racing. The novice can enter his roadster or sports coupe in a weekend rally to test his navigation and driving skill rather than his speed. In such a contest he competes against neighbors or as a member of a car club for both fun and trophies. Many other types of racing events are also available for amateurs in their home-groomed-and-tuned cars.

Still, auto racing as the general public has come to know it is largely a professional sport. It brings to mind names such as Barney Oldfield or Eddie Rickenbacker from a bygone era. Recently the names of Andretti, Unser, Gurney, Stewart, or Brabham have become famous. Even so, the line between an amateur and professional racing driver is fuzzy. If he has the machine, can pass rigid testing, and pays his entry fee, a driver is free to enter whatever races he wishes. The trail is extremely competitive, but the opportunity to become a professional always exists.

At first auto racing simply grew as automobiles became more plentiful. Such early racing was usually without plan, and its purpose was often to show off. Cars in the hands of unskilled drivers careered through town, caromed off curbings, and hung themselves on lamp poles. Traffic violations were plentiful, and a citation for speeding was sometimes considered a compliment. As automobiles became faster and more powerful, serious accidents increased. The public grew incensed over the wildness in the streets.

Europeans recognized the need to organize auto racing in the beginning of the twentieth century when road races first were run. In order to set up rules for competition, and to lay out specifications for racing cars, track standards, driver qualifications, and prizes, an association was formed in Paris, France, in 1904. Called the Federation Internationale de l'Automobile (FIA), this governing body still rules over international competition, and its regulations have been adopted throughout the world.

In the United States several auto-racing associations also sprang up. Even so, the sport remained loosely organized. Although many tracks appeared around the country, most of them did not last long.

Following World War II interest in racing picked up again. But many prewar tracks had turned into weed patches and rotting bleachers. New courses were needed, and often they were laid out on the landing strips and paved aprons of inactive military

Small foreign cars dominate amateur sports-car racing.

air bases. Fairground horse tracks and other facilities also were modified to handle auto races.

Sports-car racing surged into prominence, aided by the growing number of foreign sports cars imported into the United States. These small cars, designed for the narrow winding European roads, were ideal for racing. The MGs, Triumphs, Porsches, Fiats, Austins, and others often were used for transportation during the week, then stripped down and tuned up for weekend racing.

The Indianapolis 500 is the highlight of the championship trail.

Meanwhile, the big championship cars were back racing at Indianapolis and a few other tracks around the country. As facilities expanded and public interest grew, the National Championship Trail came into being. The title of National Champion goes to the driver who wins the most points (not necessarily the most races) during a season of some two dozen events throughout the nation.

In Europe the Grand-Prix circuit was spreading from Holland to Sicily. Heavier models of such cars as Jaguar, Mercedes-Benz, Ferrari, Aston Martin, Maserati, Cooper, Alpha Romeo, and Porsche dominated the competition. American cars like the Chevrolet Corvette and the Shelby Cobra also entered European road races. At that, the Cobra had a British developed chassis wrapped around its American motor.

But the fastest growing category of auto racing was the one organized for the souped-up stock cars. Theoretically a stock car is an automobile that one can purchase from a dealer's showroom. However, this qualification became true only for the outward appearance of the car. Beneath its hood were modi-

Stock-car competition is a popular kind of racing.

fications that created great amounts of additional horsepower.

Legend has it that stock-car racing owes at least part of its origin to the days when bootleggers beefed up their engines in order to escape pursuing revenuers. Supposedly many a creaky, battered Model-A Ford, or innocent-looking Chevy, when set upon by lawmen, roared forth with a hundred extra hidden horsepower and left the Federal agents in a cloud of smoking rubber. In fact, stock-car racing did get its start in the red clay areas of the South, where bootlegging once flourished. And although it has spread nationally, stock-car racing is still most common in this section of the country.

During this postwar period the Automobile Competition Committee of the United States (ACCUS) was set up to represent the FIA. Most racing associations aligned themselves with this committee, and they conducted virtually all the big organized racing events in the United States and Canada.

At first each association acted independently of the others. Today, however, they cooperate in order to provide drivers, promoters, and fans with the best racing.

THE RACING CIRCUITS

The United States Auto Club (USAC), which was organized in 1955, operates largely in the Midwest and Far West. Its most gala annual event is the Indianapolis 500 Memorial Day Classic. Of more recent vintage, the Pocono 500, run in Pennsylvania on Independence Day, and the California 500, run during the Labor Day weekend, have become other outstanding racing events. But the trail to the National Championship follows the winding road courses as well as the oval courses of the big 500 races.

The Indy, or championship, cars found in these races are the traditional vehicles that fans think of first when car racing is mentioned. They are the fenderless, open-wheeled, open-cockpit, single-seat racers. Aerodynamically sleek, they are built close to the ground. Most of them are powered by rear engines. Usually they carry the tag of Special on their names: Olsonite Special, STP Oil Treatment Special, Bardhal Special, or the like.

USAC also sanctions midget races and the sprint-car events. The cars in both classifications are pocket-sized models of the Indy cars, although the sprint car

Most top drivers have raced in midgets.

is somewhat larger than the midget. These cars, generally powered by front engines, remain very popular on small fairground ovals and on the few remaining dirt tracks.

In addition, USAC runs both stock-car championship races and sports-car events. Thus, the drivers in this single organization can drive a stocker one day, a sports car later in the week, and then climb into a single-seat championship car on the weekend. On a free night, they may tool a midget around an eighth-mile oval dirt track somewhere out in the country.

The National Association of Stock Car Racing (NASCAR) was formed in late 1947. Most of the events in its Grand National Championship circuit and the Grand American Challenge series are concentrated in the southeast corner of the United States. However, some of them take place as far north as Maine and as far west as California. The cars in these races are late model stock cars, generally not more than three years old. In appearance they look like cars available from any dealer, yet they are beefed up so they can reach speeds of well over 200 miles per hour.

One reason why stock-car racing has become highly popular is that every enthusiast can envision himself banking around the high-speed ovals in his

The traditional championship racing car.

own family runabout. But winning stockers are not family cars. They are given as careful grooming and tuning as an Indy racer. Their wheels never touch city streets, as they are trucked, trailered, or on occasion flown from racetrack to racetrack.

The biggest NASCAR prize for a driver is the Grand National Championship for American-made sedans. The next honor goes to the winner of the Grand American Challenge series, which is for smaller sports sedans and includes foreign-made entries. Some of these races are run on winding road courses instead of the usual oval speedways.

The largest of the racing associations is the Sports

Stockers reach over 200 miles per hour.

Car Club of America (SCCA), which dates back to 1944. Its multitude of members drive mostly in club events, and some use their cars during the week for normal transportation.

The bulk of SCCA members are amateurs, or club drivers, as they prefer to be called. Many of them aspire to become professionals. Many do not. A driver may be a student, a dentist, a car salesman, or the proprietor of a store. He enjoys the challenge of speed. He may own his own racing machine, or he may drive for a friend who owns the car and likes to tinker with it.

During the year the club sponsors hundreds of races

Club drivers race in a variety of machines.

throughout the country. In them the novice has the opportunity to pit his skill and machine against competitors with similar talent and with similar equipment. Sometimes these club races are no more than minor local contests. At other times they may be gala, well-attended events drawing cars and drivers from many parts of the country. In any case, the drivers vie for points. Those who accumulate the most get to enter national competition. The winners from different divisions of the country are invited to compete in the American Road Race of Champions. This race is divided into four major categories or twenty-one car classes. To win in any of them is the highest honor for the amateur sports-car driver.

On the other hand, there are many professionals in SCCA. Often they are the same drivers found at the Indianapolis 500 or the Daytona 24-hour endurance race. In fact, top professional racers frequently maintain memberships in every major racing association in order to be eligible for all kinds of auto racing in all parts of the world.

The three professional racing circuits of the SCCA are the Canadian-American (Can-Am) Challenge Cup series, the Trans-American (Trans-Am) Cham-

A Group 7 Can-Am sports car has an outer-world appearance.

pionship, and the Continental Championship. Each of these road-racing championships is made up of about a dozen races, which take place on different road courses scattered around the United States and Canada throughout the season.

The Can-Am races are entered by sports cars with unlimited engines, including the European Grand-Prix cars. Some have around 600 horsepower and can produce speeds up to 200 miles per hour on a straightaway. These cars are referred to generally as Group 7 sports racers. They may be powered by anything from V-8's to motorcycle engines, and they are classified according to engine size. Class A is the most powerful, Class B is the next, and so on. Group

21

7 sports racers are required to have two seats, although the one on the passenger side rarely is occupied. Car tops are optional, and the wheels must have fenders or be enclosed within the machine's body.

The championship goes to the driver who accumulates the most points during the season. Points are awarded for the first ten places in each race, and there are also cash prizes.

The Trans-Am section of SCCA racing is an endurance championship for sports sedans, both large and small. The cars are classified by their engine displacement. In the small category it is under 122 cubic inches. In the large category it is between 122 cubic inches and 305 cubic inches. Engine displacement (which can be measured by cubic centimeters, cubic inches, or liters) refers to the total volume of inner space swept by the pistons of all the cylinders during one complete stroke of each piston. Usually the greater the volume of engine displacement, the greater the power.

The smaller, more compact sedans used in the Trans-Am are known as pony cars. Many of the races are judged by the distance covered in a certain amount of time rather than by the time taken to drive a given number of miles. Usually the events last from two and a half to four hours.

In the third professional racing circuit of the SCCA, the Continental Championship, the Grand-Prix cars compete. They are the open-wheel roadsters that run in the famous European road-racing events like those at Monza, Monaco, Aintree, and Le Mans.

The bigger Continental Championship racers are called Formula A, and the smaller are called Formula B. In auto racing the word *formula* means the same as the word *class* in boat racing. The categories are established to equalize the competition among different sized cars.

Added to these various American races for championship cars, stock cars, and sports cars is the famous FIA-controlled Grand-Prix competition, which takes place on several continents. From this international circuit emerges the World's Driver Champion, the most coveted of all auto-racing titles.

In essence, these organizations enable any person with a fast car at his disposal, a feeling for speed, and the proper licenses and qualifications to find the time, place, and event to "turn the horses loose."

THE SPEED MACHINES

A racing car means different things to different people. Some think of midget racers broadsiding around a tiny oval. Others picture larger open-wheel sprint cars slinging clods of dirt as they skid around a quarter-mile fairground track.

To some a racing car is one of the large championship cars carrying the name of Lotus, Eagle, Mongoose, Coyote, or some other bench-formed body. The engine, which generally is located behind the driver, may be a Ford, Offenhauser (Offy), or Chevrolet. Hence the total machine is called a Lotus-Ford, an Eagle-Offy, or any of many possible combinations.

This type of car may be highly specialized to make only left-hand turns at such speedways as the Indianapolis, Pocono, and Ontario two-and-one-half-mile ovals, where the races always are run in a counterclockwise direction. The weight may be balanced to lean inward away from the outward thrust of the centrifugal forces generated by the frequent high-speed left turns. The tight cockpit is padded to the right to protect the driver from the almost constant bruising pressure each turn puts against his right side. Also the strength of the tires, the wheel suspension setup, and the fuel distribution are designed to meet the extra demands made on the right side of the car.

The Indy cars are the sophisticates of the racing industry. They are the biggest and most powerful of the open-wheel racers. Their turbocharged engines often are capable of generating well over 700 horsepower, twice that of a large family sedan. Turbocharging makes use of the engine exhaust to drive a fanlike turbine that sucks extra air into the engine to aid combustion and add power.

But the championship racers often weigh only

A stripped-down racer resembles a plumber's nightmare.

Fueling up a Vollstedt-Ford in Motor Speedway's famous Gasoline Alley at Indianapolis.

about 1350 pounds, half that of a family car. This combination of excess power and slight weight makes them fleet and sensitive to the touch. They can accelerate like whippets, dodge like rabbits, and produce average speeds upward of 170 miles per hour on the large ovals.

Because of their specialized design, the championship cars are ill-suited for other types of racing. They usually burn exotic fuel mixtures containing alcohol or nitromethane instead of the ordinary pump gasoline that most other race cars are restricted to. Such a hot fuel concoction can add up to forty percent extra horsepower, but it cuts down drastically on mileage and is hard on engines.

Normally these cars have about a three-speed transmission while road racers have a four- or five-speed transmission. The driver uses the first two gears only during starts and after pit stops. The rest of the race is run in high gear, the driver controlling the speed with the throttle and the brakes.

So, by and large, the championship cars are one-

The open cockpit of a championship car.

purpose vehicles. Yet their owners can make adjustments enabling the car to run races other than the Indy 500 variety. Perhaps they drop in a new engine. They change the suspension so the wheels will grip and the springs and shocks will take the uneven jolts that road courses offer. If necessary, they can change the gear box and put on different tires. In other words, they make the car fit the formula for the race to be run.

Overall weight and the number of cubic inches of

The power end of a big racing machine.

displacement in the engine are two of the major factors in a car formula. Body style, size of wheels and tires, fuel type and capacity, and the use of superchargers are other items.

Consequently, these formula cars go by such designations as Formula 1, 2, or 3, and Formula A, B, or C. The size, power, and performance capabilities of the racing cars usually decline as the code numbers get larger, or as the letters go farther into the alphabet. Although the Indy cars must adhere to certain formulas of their own, they still are not considered true formula cars, since they are not designed for road racing. In any case, even though Indy cars possibly could be called something like Formula-American, they usually are known as championship cars.

Formula 1 cars are lighter in weight than the Indy racers. Still, they are capable of equal speeds and are usually more maneuverable than the heavier machines. Since these advantages are useful on the paved ovals as well as road courses, the formula cars have been modified for track racing too. In fact, they do very well at Indianapolis, Pocono, and Ontario, to say nothing of their superiority on other tracks and road courses of the championship.

Some wedge-shaped racers like this Gerhardt-Offy resemble high-speed doorstops.

Some of these formula cars look like low-slung bathtubs on wheels. Others are wedge-shaped. They taper upward and backward from a cleaver-sharp nose to a bulky engine assembly at the rear. In some classes of formula cars the wedge may be topped off by an aerodynamic wing, or airfoil. At high speed, this wing exerts a downward pressure on the tires, helping them grip the turns. Often one of these racing cars looks like an oversized doorstop on wheels.

In contrast, the plain old stock cars of the NASCAR Grand National Championship circuit at least resemble the familiar neighborhood automobile.

These late-model, American-made sedans are the high-powered muscle machines put out by major auto manufacturers. They must weigh at least 3900 pounds gassed and ready to go. Although they use big engines, they are limited to a certain number of cubic inches of displacement, thus providing a fair basis of competition. The stockers should be a mass-produced car. That is, at least a thousand or so of the model should have been built and offered for public sale.

Despite their familiar appearance, the big stock cars have been rebuilt for the speedway. They are especially equipped from the oversized racing tires to the solidly braced top and roll cage, from radiator cap to gas cap. If not, the stocker never would be able to attain average speeds of 200 miles per hour on the high-banked super ovals, the fastest average speeds in all auto racing.

Often a stock racing car builder will purchase a body "in white." This term means a basic unpainted body having no accessories and taken directly off the manufacturer's assembly line. The builder and his mechanics make few if any changes in the shape of the car. What goes on inside, however, is another story.

They install a full roll cage to protect the driver in case of an accident. They put in special fuel tanks that contain baffled safety foam fillers to prevent serious tank ruptures and explosions. They add components and substitute parts until the car is completely altered.

Stock cars must, however, adhere to rigid specifications as laid down by the racing associations. Fuel injection systems and superchargers are not allowed. All kinds of safety devices are added. Doors are bolted or welded shut. Windows usually are removed. Interiors are stripped of panels and upholstery that might catch fire. Hoods are safety pinned. Many other changes are made. In time, a true racing machine is

Stock cars of all sizes compete in auto races.

The big stockers are speed machines.

created beneath the newly painted and decal-plastered body.

Stock cars come in assorted sizes and shapes. There are the Grand National "big bangers," which are intended for the professional builders and drivers. A most interesting division is that of the modified cars. Naturally called "modifieds," these cars show endless variety. As long as they run and conform to certain rules of design and safety, virtually any combination of engine, body, and supporting parts can be put together. Even fuel injection systems—as long as the fuel is pump gasoline—and superchargers are permitted in some classes. The cars must have self-starters, roll-bar cages, heavy-duty seat belt and shoulder harness, and a scatter shield over the flywheel and clutch assembly to stop the metal chaff in case things fly apart during a race.

If it can be made to fit, an old Chevy coupe body may sport a big supercharged Cadillac engine. In Late Model Modified cars, however, rules specify that the engine must be of the same make, although not necessarily of the same year, as the body.

The modified cars perform best on shorter ovals that are a mile or less around. They also are fine dirt machines for those tracks that are still unpaved. The class provides some of the wildest competition in all of auto racing.

Before moving up to the hotter stock cars most drivers serve an apprenticeship in the sportsman division. There the cars are lighter and less complicated. They are particularly suited to racing on courses that are a half mile or so long, such as the red clay tracks of the South. Although all types of racing machines are expensive, a good sportsman division stock car costs only about $3000 to $4000 while a championship racer, including spare engines, a transporting van, and other essential gear and supporting equipment, may cost $100,000.

For the person with more desire than money to spend on stock-car racing there is the hobby division. The main prize in hobby racing is fun, yet there are also trophies and, at times, even cash to be won. Pure amateurism scarcely is known in auto-racing circles, although some effort is made toward separating novice from professional. If nothing else, even a beginning driver hopes to earn the cost of his gas and oil now and then. In the hobby division cars are separated carefully into classes so that everyone gets a fair chance at the checkered flag.

In addition to the big championship cars and various classes of stockers, there are the sports cars. Generally a sports car is assumed to be a two-seater that is capable of carrying a passenger, but it rarely does. It may or may not have a top. It should be equipped for day and night driving and for driving in all kinds of weather. Thus, it should have fenders and necessary lights. It should be designed to run on normal pump gas instead of exotic fuel mixtures.

One category of these racers is known as production sports cars. They remain close to the version

An English Triumph represents the typical sports machine for the weekend race driver.

that comes out of the factory, although many modifications are allowed in order to boost horsepower, strengthen the machine, and assure safety.

The production sports cars are divided by the SCCA into classes A through H, based on the potential performance of different models. Included are the various Porsches, Fiats, Ferraris, Corvettes, Triumphs, Alfa Romeos, Datsuns, and many others. Indeed, this group of vehicles is by far the largest in sports-car racing as it is the most accessible to the beginner.

An exact definition of a sports car is hard to state.

The car must have good brakes, positive steering, proper wheel suspension, fenders, and other normal items, but the same is true of any car. Perhaps the only way to identify a sports car is to check its performance. If it can take the curves faster than other cars, if it can race up hills, accelerate on the straights, and if it handles well on either dry or wet pavement or on cobblestones, the car may make a sports racer. If it can go faster than another car of similar weight and power, it certainly may be considered a sports racing car.

A majority of competitive sports cars are foreign-

A variety of small sports cars take the esses on a road course.

A groomed and tuned Mustang.

built. American manufacturers specialize in big, comfortable, high-powered family automobiles while foreign companies excel in producing the small speedsters so well adapted to the tortuous network of narrow roads over which most sports-car competition takes place. There are, of course, a few exceptions, such as the Chevrolet Corvette, the Shelby GT350, and the American Motors AMX. Otherwise, sports-car races are dominated by foreign-made machines.

Among the other categories of sports cars is the compact sedan division with three classes ranging from minicars to Mustangs. There also are classes of formula sports cars similar to yet different from

A Group 7 road racer is sheer power on wheels.

the international formula cars. These racers are typically open-wheel, open-cockpit cars of varying sizes. They are powered by an assortment of engines ranging from Volkswagens to much heavier American production power plants. The smaller of these broad-tired sports cars are the "buzzing hornets" so often seen and heard on sports racing courses.

Still another sports-car category is the Group 7 sports racing class. These cars have enclosed wheels and two seats. Otherwise, there is little resemblance between them and a normal automobile. Many are one-of-a-kind, home-built specials, while others are high-powered Lolas, Lotuses, McLarens, Porsches,

39

Alfa Romeos, or such. Some use stabilizing wings and assorted aerodynamic spoilers to increase traction on the roadway.

Despite the numerous styles, classes, and categories of racing cars, each is still made up of the basic components of any automobile. It has a body mounted on a frame. (Unless it is monocoque, in which case the body and the frame are a single stress-molded unit, often called a "tub.") From this body project four wheels. They are securely held by a suspension system made up of hinged rods, axles, springs, and shock absorbers. When suspended prop-

Racing rubber comes in all shapes and sizes
to fit the varied demands of cars and tracks.

erly, the wheels absorb road jolts, take the pressure of high-speed cornering, and otherwise keep the racing machine stable.

The broad wheels hold special, broad tires. They are lightweight but strong, and sometimes the treads are a foot and a half wide. The more rubber that contacts the ground, the better the traction, and traction is a critical factor in auto racing. Hence, good safe tires are considered to be a most important part of a race car.

Then there are the brakes so essential to slowing the car or stopping it when necessary. Brakes are used frequently in all forms of auto racing, particularly on the road courses. Most racing cars use oversized disc brakes, which have proven far superior to drum brakes.

To make the whole machine go requires a complicated chain of power. This so-called power train begins at the engine and extends through the transmission and clutch assemblies, and on to the axles on which the wheels turn. Everything must be oiled, fed fuel, cooled, exhausted of spent gases, and prevented from blowing up under stress.

With such a car one can be competitive.

ROAD COURSES AND OVALS

There are enormous numbers and varieties of auto racetracks throughout the world. In the United States most towns of even moderate size have some kind of a graded oval or a winding road course plotted out on which local hot rodders can turn their speedsters loose. However, many such races and the tracks on which they are run are neither sanctioned nor safe. They are known in racing circles as outlaw operations. Few prominent drivers attend them. In fact, racing associations forbid their members' driving on such tracks.

Even some of the tracks supported by the associations lack proper conveniences and safety conditions for both drivers and fans. Yet, most are being improved.

Many a fairground paddock or small horse-racing track has been converted into an auto-racing track. Perhaps it is a mere quarter mile of unbanked dirt, perhaps longer. When smoothed off and wet down, it can accommodate a field of midget racers, sprint cars, ministocks, and other small race-tuned machines. Indeed, races run on these dirt tracks usually are crowd pleasers. In the uncertain going, the cars slide broadside into the corners, throw up rooster tails of dirt, and snarl in and out of the short straights. In such close quarters fifty miles per hour seems like a hundred or more. Wheels scrape and fenders bump. Still, the speeds are sufficiently low so that the consequences are seldom serious.

Then there are the larger banked dirt tracks. Often they are clay tracks that have been graded and packed until the surface is almost like pavement. Some of these ovals are a mile or more around. They attract stockers, formula cars, and even at times the larger championship cars.

Bird's-eye view of Indianapolis Motor Speedway on race day.

But dirt tracks are becoming scarce. Fans who have seen televised races on first-class ovals and road courses are less willing to stand around behind rickety fences eating dust and tolerating other spectator discomforts that are encountered so often around dirt tracks. As a result, the number of larger, paved tracks is increasing.

Actually far more racing cars compete on winding road courses than on ovals. For spectator convenience, these courses usually are closed so the racers circle periodically back through the start-finish line, each circuit measuring a couple of miles or so.

Such road circuits vary greatly in length and terrain. The Grand-Prix course of Holland is about two and one-half miles long. It winds in and out and around grass-covered sand dunes, which usually are being buffeted by cold winds off the North Sea. A similar length Grand-Prix course in South Africa is virtually level, but the track is laid out with sharp corners and difficult serpentine esses.

The Grand Prix of Monaco is run on a tortuous two-mile course made up of dangerously narrow streets that dip and climb along the seaside resort. One of the toughest of the Grand-Prix courses is the Nürburgring in Germany. The Ring, as it is called, consists of fourteen miles of writhing roadway through hilly and heavily forested countryside. When racing on the rain-plagued course, cars frequently become airborne as they top a rise at high speed. In all there are more than 170 curves and sharp left and right bends to negotiate. The Ring puts both driver and car to a stern test.

The Targa Florio of Sicily is another murderous course. There are nearly forty-five bone-jarring, nerve-shattering miles in a single lap, eleven of which make up a race. The Targa Florio includes such rugged hills and sharp corners that average speeds seldom exceed seventy miles per hour, which is extremely slow for Grand-Prix racing. Only the most

Road courses often wind through scenic countryside.

tenacious drivers and the best built cars can last through a few laps of the Targa Florio roller coaster.

So there is no standard Grand-Prix racing circuit. Length and route are carefully chosen in order to provide drivers and cars with a serious challenge. At the same time the courses must have convenient locations for pits and grandstands and midcourse spectator vantage points. Most of all, great consideration must be given to the safety of both fans and participants.

The most famous of the European sports-car races is the Twenty-Four Hours of Le Mans. The Le Mans course is a maze of two-lane highways. It combines dips and swoops, sharp corners guarded by bales of straw, sinuous esses, and several long straights on which the throttles can be pushed to the floor. During the twenty-four-hour endurance race, teams of drivers exchange turns at the wheel. Sometime during the day-and-night span, the drivers usually face the extra hazard of rain.

North America boasts Grand-Prix road courses in such places as Sebring, Florida; Riverside, California; Watkins Glen, New York; Edmonton, Alberta, Canada; and a dozen or so more. They wind over

Stock cars racing on the speedway oval at Daytona Beach.

all sorts of terrain and can be laid out on roadway systems that are established already.

Still, recently in the United States a growing number of so-called super speedways have been constructed. Where possible, they include both an oval and a road course, which branches off it. Florida's Daytona International Speedway, the site of the famous Daytona 500 stock-car races and a variety of other events, is such a racing plant. It has a two-and-one-half-mile, high-banked trioval. A trioval is a sort of *D*-shaped oval on which the main, or grandstand,

47

straight bows out a bit. By blocking off certain corners and opening up other stretches, the infield can be set up for paved road courses of three different lengths.

The Michigan International Speedway, the Texas International Speedway, and several others belong in the super speedway category.

One of the newer of these plants is the Ontario Motor Speedway, located about forty miles east of Los Angeles. OMS, or the Big O, as it is sometimes called, has been set up as a deliberate imitation of Indianapolis, a sort of Indianapolis West.

The two-and-one-half-mile, squared oval at Ontario is the same length and shape as Indy, although it is steeply banked in places. In addition, the design of the Ontario race facilities improves on that of the aging Indianapolis plant. Whereas the Indy oval lies flat on the terrain, enabling spectators to catch only fleeting glimpses of the racing action, the Ontario track is raised above the infield. Also the back straight is elevated thirty feet higher than the front straight. Thus, the entire race is visible to those in the grandstands and bleachers, and partially to those in the infield areas.

The Ontario Motor Speedway ranks high among modern race plants.

The squared oval at Ontario is made up of a long straight on either side of the field, plus a short straight, or short chute, at each end. Four curves, or corners, tie the chutes together. Each curve is about a quarter mile long from the point of entry to the beginning of the next straight. Each short chute is about 600 feet. This distance is just long enough for a driver to get his car straightened out, take a new grip on the wheel, and prepare to enter the next corner. Each of the long straights is 3300 feet. The one running in front of the grandstand is the main straight, or chute. The other, on the far side of the infield, is the back straight, or chute. The entire track has a thick asphalt surfacing.

The pit area stretches along the main straight. It is separated from the track itself by a low concrete wall. The pit road leading into it branches off the main speedway coming out of Turn 4, the final turn before reaching the start-finish line.

The pits themselves are simply marked-off and numbered segments of parking space in back of the low cement guard wall. At race time each space is loaded with the parts and supplies, the fuel storage tanks, and whatever else the pit crew feels it may need to keep the race car going during the full course of the contest.

The famed Victory Circle is located directly behind the pit area at Ontario. It is a slanted ramp, tilted

Mechanics, crewmen, officials, and their paraphernalia surround a driver while making a pit stop.

toward the grandstand for the convenience of the spectators. There the victor basks in his brief moment of glory.

Behind the Victory Circle is the manufacturers' building and six long, rectangular, aluminum garages. Each one is partitioned into eighteen stalls big enough to accommodate a racing machine and its working crew.

This garage area is similar to the famous Gasoline Alley at Indianapolis, although in many ways it is much improved. Until recently the garages of most racetracks have been off limits to spectators. Now, however, many of them have been opened to the public at a small extra charge.

The garage area, Victory Circle, start-finish line, and main grandstand at Ontario.

In the heat of a long championship race keeping track of each car's position and its standing is very difficult. In past races at other tracks there even have been bitter arguments over who won what place in the competition. Despite the best efforts of human monitors, confusion can result from a crash, a yellow warning light, or a jumble of pit stops. Cars can get lost in the shuffle easily, and mistakes made in their lap counts.

To do away with this shortcoming, Ontario has installed racing's first computerized scoring system. Each car is equipped with a small radio transmitting device. A wire embedded in the track picks up the particular coded signal of the car as it completes a lap. Thus, there is no way a lap can be added or subtracted, and everyone knows which car is ahead of another.

A central computer instantly flashes the result on the three readily visible sixty-five-foot scoring pylons spotted around the infield. This scoring system readily proved its worth from the very first day of its use during the inaugural California 500 in 1970. On the hot, windy day racers were banging walls, blowing engines, and scrambling in and out of the pits, often in mass confusion. While cars kept dropping out, the computerized system never missed a digit, and it kept track of where each car was at any time.

Like all the new super speedways, the Ontario infield includes a raised and winding Grand-Prix track. This road circuit is completely self-contained within the oval and does not extend into adjoining countryside as is true of some other tracks. Thus all of the action is plainly visible from the grandstands. The course can be altered to different lengths, the longest of which is three and two tenths miles and has twenty turns. Typically the road course at Ontario has no Turn 13.

To complete its versatility, Ontario can convert its broad pit road into a quarter-mile drag strip for drag racers.

In order to operate profitably, most speedways offer all kinds of racing. Only the Indianapolis Motor Speedway confines itself to a single race a year. Other tracks plan a broad program of events, so that their facilities are used frequently. One week their schedules will feature the open-wheel championship cars in a 500-mile race. A few weeks later a field of late model stock sedans may take to the asphalt. On still another weekend, the strident buzzing of Formula A, B, C, F (Ford), Vee (stock Volkswagen engine), or Super Vee (modified VW engine) cars fills the air. On some days there are doubleheaders to please the fans. A championship car contest may be followed by a stock-car race.

Often the track is turned over to the local licensed talents, so they can determine who is the latest speed demon of the neighborhood. At such events, the crowds may be small, but they have fun and feel the competition keenly.

All these oval tracks and road circuits make up a worldwide network that show automobile racing at its exciting best.

Every racetrack emphasizes safety.

THE DRIVERS

The true driver is not happy unless he is racing, no matter what the vehicle handy. An amusing example occurred once on the morning of a big race. During the long wait one of the drivers spotted several small minitractors nearby. Normally they were used to pull the racing machines between the pit area and the garages.

"Race you around the paddock," the driver shouted suddenly, making a beeline for the nearest tractor.

Immediately accepting the challenge, several other drivers ran for tractors. With whoops and hollers, they kicked life into the engines and soon were barreling around the paddock at some six or seven miles per hour.

Cutting a corner too short, one of the drivers hooked a wheel on the edge of a garage. His rig flipped over, and he scraped a large patch of skin from his leg. Had the accident been more serious, he would have missed out driving in the big race for which he had been preparing and practicing.

Of all the qualifications a race driver must have, dedication and desire top the list. Yet his success and survival depend upon many additional characteristics as well.

A race driver must be brave. However, overeager "hot dogs" usually burn themselves out quickly. They blow engines or hang cars on the wall so frequently that car owners shy away from them. Only through much practice and long experience does a driver learn the proper ratio of caution to courage that will bring him unscathed out of tight situations. He never drives over his head. Yet, under proper control, he sometimes pushes himself to the edge of disaster for

A driver prepares to take his machine onto the track.

the sake of winning. He must be confident, but never careless or cocky.

Certainly race driving is a highly physical endeavor. The driver's senses must be alert, for during a race his eyes, ears, and nose need to pick up important signals. His hands and feet remain constantly busy. In the course of a 500-mile race, a driver's arms and hands may give out unless he has trained like an Olympic athlete to strengthen them.

Furthermore, he must be able to endure the pounding vibration and screaming of engines under incredible stress. He must tolerate the searing heat in the cockpit while swathed in an unventilated fire suit, protective gloves, a stifling face mask, and a heavy helmet. He must withstand the added G-forces pushing him one way or another as he makes high-speed turns and slams into the high-banked corners of the oval speedways.

A driver usually is a better than average athlete. He has coordination and rhythm. With his feet he continually operates the three controls—clutch pedal, brake pedal and throttle—located deep in the footwell of the racer. He is able to react at about the same instant he decides which control to use.

A driver's ears are attuned to his engine. He can feel the extra vibration caused by overstraining. He can recognize the sound of a faulty plug or an overheating piston. He can tell by the hum of his tires whether the tread is wearing out and whether he should make a pit stop to change rubber.

A driver may be a "charger" or a "stroker." The best driver is a little of both. At one point he will

Drivers wrapped up in "racing metal."

charge through a field of cars, perhaps scraping paint on both sides. On another occasion, with the lead well in hand, he may decide to slow down, or stroke it, thus saving his engine and assuring his victory. The smart driver drives just fast enough to win.

Many drivers do not own their own racing machines, but drive for someone else. Thus, they are not required to tinker with the cars. However, any good driver gets involved in the mechanics of his machine. Invariably, sometime before a race, he will be found in the garage with the crew, either helping or observing as they prepare the car for competition.

A driver also must study aspects of racing that have little to do with the actual driving, but everything to do with winning races. For instance, he must learn the layout of each track in order that he may drive to a plan. Whether the race is over an oval or a road course, he must establish his racing groove, or line, which will take him around the track in the shortest, quickest, and safest way.

By practice and observation the driver learns how wide to take the straights. He establishes points of reference, so he knows just where to lift his foot from the throttle and touch the binders, or brakes, and where to switch back from brake pedal to accelerator. Within legal limits, he figures out how to cut corners as close as possible and establish the shortest, fastest line around the track.

A sincere driver often will work up a map, or "blueprint," which shows the exact shift points for each turn and bend of a road course. He sets up a scenario of the best tachometer reading for revolutions per minute to use at each corner and with each shift of gears. Just as no two racetracks are alike, no two drivers use the same plan to run a track.

Different tracks usually require different adjustments on the racing car. Perhaps stiffer suspension or broader tires are called for. A new set of gears or tighter steering may be needed before the car will run on the track properly. The good driver involves himself in these preparations.

There is no easy way to become a race driver. Many good ones start out jockeying small sports cars and stock cars around local dirt ovals. With success, they graduate into the racing sedans or the small formula classes. From there they move up to the big stockers or Formula 1 and championship car competition.

YELLOW (RED STRIPE)
Oil on the course.

GREEN
The course is clear. Start.

BLACK
Stop at starting line.

RED
The race has been stopped.

YELLOW
Caution . . . hold your position.

BLUE (ORANGE STRIPE)
You are being overtaken; give way.

WHITE
Emergency vehicle on course.

CHECKERED
Congratulations, you finished the race.

The basic racing flags.

On the other hand, a novice may enroll in one of several reputable schools of high-performance driving. There he will learn how to drive competitively. For example, he is instructed to drive defensively even when pushing toward victory.

One of the first things a beginner learns is the flag and light code. Green is used for the start, yellow for caution, and black for a return to the pits because of an oil leak or other hazardous condition. A red flag or light stops the race. The checkered flag, of course, means victory.

In order to compete in sanctioned racing events, a driver must be at least twenty-one years old, have passed a thorough physical examination, and possess a racing license. The fellow who has his novice permit, however, must still earn a regional license and, in time, a national license if he hopes to enter the big races. A holder of a national competition license may apply for an FIA driver's license, which makes him eligible for certain categories of racing worldwide.

Each association—NASCAR, SCCA, USAC, and others—have definite membership policies and licensing programs that prevent unapproved drivers from participating in sanctioned races. These licenses are not interchangeable. So most professional drivers carry several to be ready for any driving opportunity.

The very essence of the race is danger. A driver understands the chances he takes, but doesn't let himself think too much about them. If he gets in an accident or witnesses a nerve-shattering raceway disaster —and few drivers escape either or both—he knows that the best antidote is to get back in a racer and drive again as soon as possible.

If he continues to relish the acrid smell of hot oil, the salty taste of sweat, and the ear-splitting roar of straining engines, he has a proper dedication to his profession. If the very sight of a racetrack and the cars and the people that go with it sends the blood coursing more rapidly through his veins, he is in his element. He has made a good choice.

A championship driver relies on
confidence, courage, and caution.

THE WRENCHES

Just as the visible part of an iceberg is held up by a mass many times its weight lying beneath the surface of the sea, a professional race driver could not exist without the support of his garage mechanics. The big cars, whether the sleek championship types or high-powered stock sedans, usually are cared for by a chief mechanic, aided perhaps by a small corps of "wrenches," as mechanics often are called.

Except for the major tracks, the so-called garage areas are little more than a paddock or parking lot onto which the participants tow their racing machines. After unloading them from trailers or trucks, drivers and crew set up temporary housekeeping during the race meet. Overnight a small village of campers, house trailers, or tents springs up in an area adjacent to the racetrack. Behind almost every one of these temporary quarters is a racing machine of one type or another.

This paddock area is one of the more interesting sights at a weekend race meet. There the cars are tuned up for the competition. The area may be divided into spaces for particular classes of cars. One

Cars and enthusiasts crowd the paddock area during a race meet.

row may consist of Formula Fords. Next to it may be a row or two of Class B or C sedans. Other blocks of space will be occupied by Formula A, B, and C's. On still another patch of pavement in a corner one may find the heavier Can-Am sports-racing machines crowded together.

Thus, drivers, owners, and mechanics of similar cars can share experiences and shop gossip, all of which comes under the general heading of bench racing. Often they help each other by doing wrench work or exchanging parts. In fact, despite the all-out rivalry that takes place as soon as the race begins, auto-racing people take great pride in helping one another when they are off the track.

Among the big car classes, the actual setting up of the machine for a race is entirely the responsibility of the chief mechanic. He oversees everything that goes on in the garage and usually in the pits. In addition to a salary, the chief wrench receives a percentage of any winnings. His expertise may be general enough so he can get the machine race ready himself. Or he

A car is completely stripped down and set up again before a championship race.

may call upon separate specialists in carburetion, ignition, suspension, and braking.

In the dark early morning hours before a big 500-mile race, an amazing amount of work remains to be done. In one stall an orange racer is up on blocks, with all wheels removed and the body lid standing in a corner. Nuts, bolts, and rods lie around on the floor. There is no sign of panic among the mechanics, although they will have to put everything together

An engine virtually is rebuilt
before it goes into a racing machine.

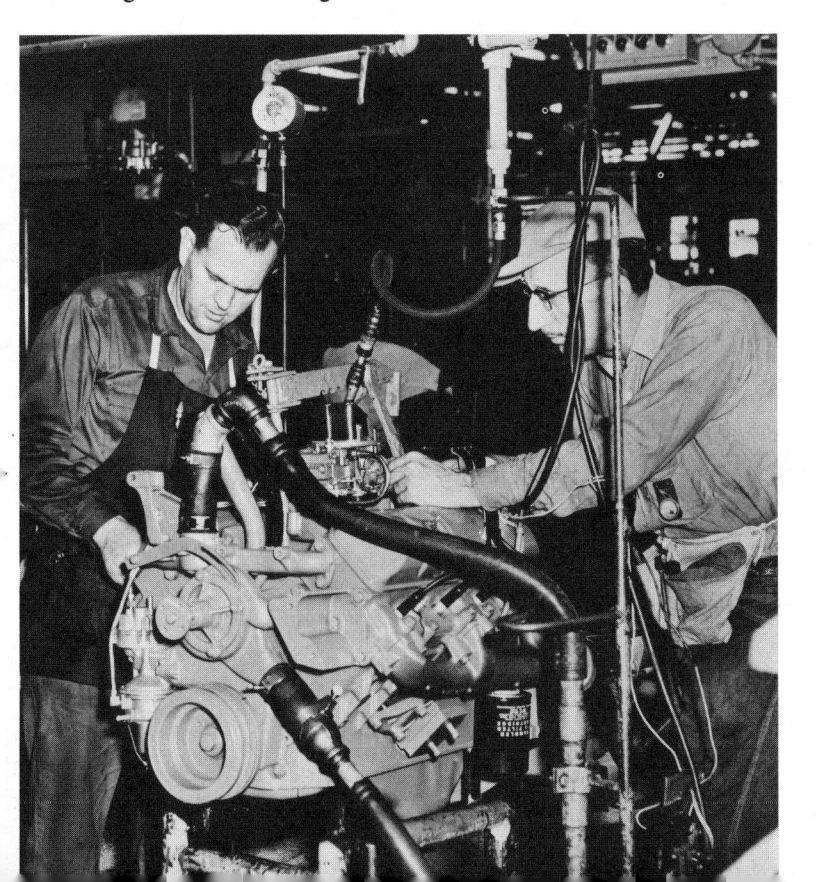

Tires and wheels are balanced before a race.

again and go through a weigh-in and technical inspection before the approaching deadline for the race.

In another garage, while the driver sits on a box in a corner trying not to show his anxiety, mechanics drop a new engine into a chassis and begin connecting tubes, wires, and more rods. Days of normal work are being compressed into scant hours.

Meanwhile, at still another garage, the chief wrench peers at the morning sky. He goes out and makes a brief study of track conditions. Then he ponders which tires he should put on the racing machine. He has the basic choices of wet, dry, or intermediate tires, depending on the different rubber compound used. Since proper tires are as important as the engine, they cannot be chosen by hit or miss. Each tire has an inner liner for safety and has been painstakingly balanced.

Safety rubber fuel cells, which are covered with metal pods, are used on many types of cars.

In time, the wrenches have the car properly set up. Engine, gears, suspension, weight distribution, and drivers are attuned to each other. If any of these factors is out of balance, the car will perform poorly. Now if something goes wrong, the mechanics will blame it on a faulty Johnson Rod, the mythical part used by racing people as a scapegoat.

At this point the chief mechanic fires up the engine and calls the driver over. Before leaving the garage, a thorough check is made of all safety equipment. The fire-resistant driving suit is inspected from tight cuffs and collar to zippers and fasteners. The crash helmet is adjusted for comfort as well as safety. A new five-layer plastic face shield is set in place. Should oil spatters, dirt, or other impurities fog the driver's vision during the race, he can reach up and peel off the top layer, so the shield is clean again. The crew checks the fire extinguisher that is required in every racing machine. Some of them operate automatically, triggered by a heat-sensing device.

Normally the mechanics also work in the pits. In major professional races, however, specially trained crews may handle the pit chores. In either case, a pit crew diligently practices its functions of refueling,

Mechanics often double as pit crewmen.

changing tires, adjusting engines, and wiping windshields long before a race. With experience their movements develop the timing and grace of a smooth, if brief, ballet.

Pit crews vary in numbers at different tracks and in different classes of races. Generally a limited number of crewmen are allowed over the low pit wall during a pit stop. Perhaps the limit is four, perhaps five or six. To eliminate danger and confusion, any additional crewmen must perform their functions from behind the pit wall. An engine expert may lean over to listen to the engine's tune. Another crewman may poke a cold soft drink out toward the driver on the end of a stick. Still another at the fuel storage tank will control the liquid flowing through heavy hoses to the racer's tanks.

Not far away will be a scorer officially designated to keep track of a particular car. In addition there is the pit-board man, busily erasing or chalking messages that he flashes regularly during the race to the driver.

The most important concern of the pit crew is to avoid confusion. As a true example of what can happen when things get out of hand, there is the case where a cup of brake fluid inadvertently was thrust out toward the driver. Thinking it a cold soda, he gulped it down. He had to be taken from the car and rushed to the hospital to have his stomach pumped. Obviously, after months of practice and preparation, that race was over for the driver, the crew, and the entire team.

So the mechanics, whether working in the garage or in the pits, are as essential to the winning of a race as the car itself.

THE RACE

The atmosphere is festive, the crowd large. Many people have arrived the day before, crowding into hotels and motels or sleeping in their cars and campers. A few even queued up during the night, huddled in blankets or sleeping bags, waiting for the gates to open in the morning.

The dew is hardly off the infield grass as the championship cars are towed out to their respective pits. Bands begin to play, and soon what seems like all the colored balloons in the world are turned loose. They rise in a great cluster in front of the grandstand, start to spread out, then slant off into the sky in the grip of the morning breeze. You and your crew watch them anxiously. You hope the breeze doesn't stiffen during the race and cause problems on the track.

Before long the cars are rolled onto the starting grid. Each takes the position it earned during the earlier days of four-lap qualifying runs. The front pole, or inside position of the first row, is highly favored and goes to the car with the lowest qualifying time. Two more positions—center and outside—complete the row. Altogether there are eleven rows of

The weigh-in preceding a race.

three, each position determined by the car's fastest qualifying time. You are Row 4, outside. Not the best, but not bad.

The chief steward climbs into the pace car and sets out to make a final inspection of the track. He nods approvingly as he completes the circuit. The color bearers make their entry. The band plays the national anthem, and the audience joins in.

As each driver is introduced over the P.A. system, he squeezes into the tight cockpit of his car. When your name is announced, you lift your hand momentarily in recognition of the applause, then slide carefully into the hammocklike seat of your racer. You are lying more than sitting, and the cockpit cowl fits around you like a collar.

After a crewman helps secure your seat belt and shoulder harness, you test the straps and adjust yourself as comfortably as possible. You reach straight ahead and grasp the small *D*-shaped steering wheel at the ten and two o'clock positions. You try out the clutch, throttle, and brake pedals unseen in the narrow cone of the footwell. You can feel them readily through the sensitive thin soles of your high leather boxing shoes.

The driver gets into his
finely tuned racing machine.

A crewman fires up the engine with a portable electric starter.

Now the crewman zips the collar of your fireproof racing coveralls tight around your neck. You slip the fabric face mask up over your chin, set your goggles, and pull on your gloves. You peer ahead thoughtfully at Turn 1 of the low-banked oval on which this annual classic race is run.

"Gentlemen," the familiar words ring out across the speedway, "start your engines!"

A mechanic inserts the metal shaft of the portable battery-powered starter into the rear-engine socket. You let your chief mechanic work the throttle on the engine as the starter spins. He is much better ac-

76

quainted with the engine's vagaries than you are. Finally the engine coughs to life amid the acrid fumes of methanol and high-octane gas.

The pace car already is positioned in front of the field of racing machines. Now it begins to move away from the start-finish line. Helped by shoves from their crew, the racers get under way and follow.

The first lap is a parade, a time to show off to the crowd the finest high-speed auto machinery in the world. The mechanics have trouble getting one racer fired up. But at last it starts, and the driver takes advantage of the ceremonial lap to catch up with the field.

Then, with the pace car leading them into the second lap, the cars begin jocking seriously for starting position. The drivers try to hold to their proper place in the eleven rows of three abreast, but the cars growl and buck to be turned loose.

Coming out of Turn 4, the pace car suddenly darts into the pit lane. You can hear the growing intensity of the engine sounds as, sensing a good start, each driver begins pushing down on his throttle. Also you faintly hear the growing wave of sound from thousands of excited voices. The cars ahead look good, and you assume that those behind are all in place.

Then it's there—the green flag waving vigorously from the starter's stand. At the instant of its first flick, you shove the throttle all the way home. The passing wind rumbles in your ears like a blanket being shaken. As speed increases, the sound becomes a roar.

Going into Turn 1 on the first lap is a crucial phase. The traffic is the heaviest it ever will be. But now is the time to establish your position, to pick up a few places if possible. So you let your machine ride high on the outside coming down the straight. Then, flashing a quick glance into your rearview mirror, you cut for the inside of the turn. You howl through it, ac-

Championship cars string out on a corner.

celerate into the short chute, and sweep down once more through Turn 2. The razor sharpness of your reactions and timing pay off. You have improved your position in the pack from twelfth to ninth.

Round and round, you get settled in for the 200-lap grind. In the beginning the traction is good, and you keep charging the corners, picking up two more positions by the twenty-fifth lap. During that time you have been setting up your groove carefully. Already the combined tires of the racers are beginning to paint a broad, dark path around the oval. It swings out toward the wall of the straights and curves down to the very edge of the infield at the corners.

As lap falls behind lap, you keep a close eye on your pit board whenever you streak down the main straight. You identify your board from the others, because it has your name written on the top. On one lap you catch the message *Pos-6,* your pit-board man's way of telling you that you have moved up into sixth place. Then, a couple of laps later, you get the information *L-45,* meaning you have completed forty-five laps.

In another ten minutes the pit board reads *Pit-3L.* The crew is calling you in to make a pit stop after the next three laps. You don't argue. They know

The pit board informs the driver
of the progress of a race.

better than you what the fuel and tire situation is. Your chief mechanic has scheduled the three mandatory pit stops exactly so that you will finish the race with at least a slight skin of rubber left on the tires and a quart or two of fuel in the tanks.

Besides a few seconds of rest will be welcome. The vibration of the race has jarred your senses. The heat in the cockpit stifles you. Your arms and legs ache from the constant effort of keeping the raging machine under control.

Trying to lose as little time as possible, you come

coasting into the pit lane fast. You hold off on your brakes as much as you can and keep wide of several other cars also making pit stops. At the last moment you swerve in to your small patch of marked-off concrete. You hope you can come to a full stop in its short length. If you overshoot it, you are obliged to go all the way around the track again.

The pit crew, except for the crew chief, is poised behind the low wall. They are grasping tires, hose nozzles, jacks, and grounding wire. Each man is ready to spring into action the moment you stop.

The crew chief himself is already over the wall. He

The pit crew performing its urgent tasks.

stands firmly, legs spread, directly in front of you. He seems to be courting danger deliberately as you bear down upon him, still trying not to lose too much speed in the approach. You use your binders sparingly, waiting until your front wheels are almost on the crew chief's toes before you step down hard on the brake pedal. Immediately the rest of the permitted crew tumbles over the pit wall with tires, serpentine three-inch fuel hoses, and other paraphernalia.

While the two tiremen quickly check the right-hand rubber—always the first to wear on counterclockwise ovals—another crewman clamps a ground wire to the

Wrestling a heavy fuel hose is not easy.

car frame. In this way he minimizes the chance of a static spark setting off a fuel flare-up. Then he stands by with a jack in case the tiremen signal that rubber needs to be changed.

Meanwhile, the fuelers man the two heavy hoses protruding from the storage tank located behind the pit wall. The right-hand fueler has the longer hose. He has to wrestle it around the front of the racer without knocking the tiremen down. Then he must get the aircraft nozzle firmly seated and locked into the right-hand tank. The left fueler does the same thing.

Any error by either man can result in a leak. Should

Trouble in the pits.

the high-potency fuel spill on hot exhaust pipes or even on the searing disc brakes, a tragic conflagration can occur. A safety-patrol man stands by alertly, ready with his fire extinguisher in case of trouble.

Precious seconds tick off. Each one might well be calculated in thousands of dollars, the difference between one finishing position and the next. You fidget, wanting the crew to hurry up, but knowing they are doing their best.

The crew chief wipes off the low wind screen in front of you. As fuel pours into the two tanks that bracket the cockpit, the tireman signals for a change of right front rubber. Even while the jack is being slipped into place, the tireman hammers off the spinner hub and removes the wheel and tire. As the old wheel comes off, a new one is jammed onto the axle.

You are happy to see that none of the crewmen are digging wrenches out of their toolboxes. There is no time allowed during pit stops for anything but the most minor adjustments on the racing machine.

Still more seconds tick off . . . 15, 16, 17, an eternity.

Then suddenly the ballet reverses itself. In a single motion the jack man lowers the new wheel onto the asphalt. The crewman at the fuel storage tank slams the main feed valve closed. As though by signal, the fuelers uncouple their hoses and snap the tank caps shut.

. . . 19, 20 seconds.

The fuelers tumble back over the wall with their hoses, but the other men wait momentarily. The crew chief's eyes sweep over the scene, as the man at the rear unsnaps the ground wire. His decision is instantaneous.

Whap, whap! You feel the firm slap of his hand on your helmet. "Go!" he shouts. "Go!"

Crewmen push an Eagle-Offy from the pits.

You feed throttle and snap out the clutch. All remaining hands shove to help get you under way again. Soon you're rolling down the pit lane and back onto the track.

The official scorer behind the pit wall checks his watch. "Twenty-one seconds," he announces.

Everyone looks pleased. No record, but good time for changing a wheel, dumping nearly seventy-five gallons of fuel into the tanks, and checking all that needs to be checked.

As the race progresses, more and more cars drop out. One throws a clutch. Another burns a bearing. An oil line breaks, and the race is slowed down under a yellow flag until the mess is cleaned up. A fuel nozzle fouls up during the pit stop of a Brabham-Ford, and before the fire is dowsed the car is out of commission. Someone else blows an engine in the sixty-fifth lap.

Then, as you go into Turn 4 of the sixty-ninth lap, the driver directly ahead of you waits too long to ease off on the throttle. Skidding on the remnants of the oil slick, he "loses it." You hold your breath as he spins out. He turns once, twice, then hangs his car on the wall, only to bounce off and go careering down

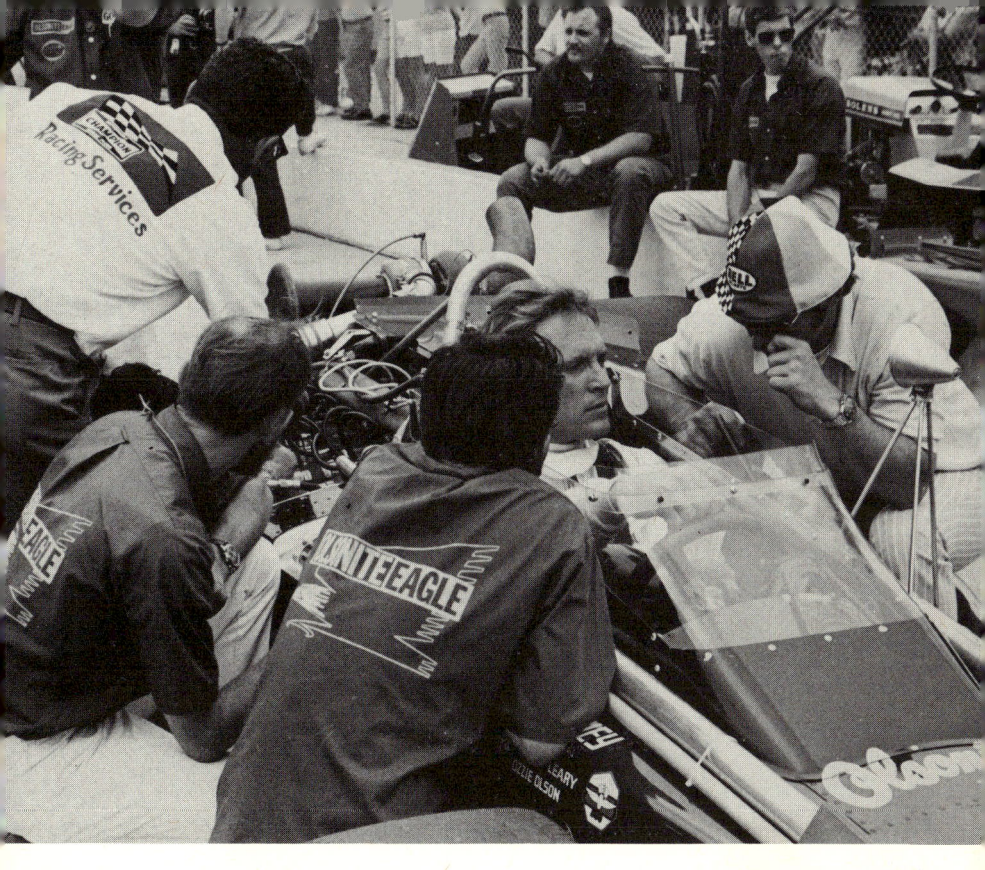

When a driver removes his helmet he indicates
the race is prematurely over for him.

the banked corner toward the infield. For a moment he is directly in front of you. There is nothing you can do, but aim for him and trust he won't be there when you arrive at the spot. Any quick evasive movement on your part will put you in the same predicament as his.

A racer spins out and ends up
in an infield cloud of dust.

Cutting low and holding your line, you brush past. Out of the corner of your eye you see him rock to a stop on the infield turf. He is safe, but out of the action. You are in fifth place.

By now you are well settled into the race and have your groove picked out. Like each of the other remaining drivers, you feel that your line around the track is the shortest and best there is. You accelerate down past the start-finish line, judging by your tachometer that you are hitting a good 200 miles per hour. Coming into Turn 1, you start backing off on the throttle while giving the brakes a gentle touch. Easy, though.

Power will get you through more corners than brakes. It keeps traction on your tires and makes them stick to the asphalt.

You aim down at the white line marking the inside edge of the oval. You try to straighten out the corner. You slant down from the outer wall, cutting diagonally across the track until your left tires are on the line. Then, as you come out of the corner, fighting the centrifugal force that pushes you against the right side of the cockpit, you shove the throttle down once more. The acceleration propels you into the straight short chute, between the first and second turns, and up toward the wall again.

You fall in behind the car running fourth. He is going all out, too. You have just enough horses to nudge in close to his rear end. The vacuum behind his car helps suck you along. This maneuver, which is called "drafting," gives you a little extra throttle reserve that you can use at the right moment.

He knows you're there, but can do nothing about you without compromising his position in the race. So you wait, wondering what is going on in his mind, wondering if you can outthink him. He is not going to let you pass if he can stop you.

Going into Turn 3, you let your car drift into the corner. You deliberately hold it high, hoping he will think you are going to try passing on the outside. You feint slightly outward to lend substance to this possibility. Then you duck down and slingshot past, taking him on the inside. Now you are in fourth place.

Shortly after your second pit stop, a few laps into the second half of the race, the car holding number two position cracks an oil tank. He is immediately black flagged into the pits, and out of the race. Snake-bit again, as the saying goes. Everyone moves up a position. You to third.

The field has both thinned down and strung out. Of the original thirty-three starters only seventeen remain. You have lapped several of them. But all of the cars will hold on as long as possible. In big races even the last car to finish earns a cash prize.

When your eyes aren't scanning the engine instruments, they are focused on the duel ahead between the first two cars. They are "dicing" for the lead, roaring down the straightaways wheel to wheel. One overtakes the other, then skids slightly in the corner and is overtaken in turn. Not only is the win at stake. The drivers are fighting for lap money, which may

Two racers "dicing" wheel-to-wheel for the lead.

go as high as $250 for the leader of each lap. It can add up.

But you are after the bigger prize. You don't alter your plan. On the 157th lap you are called in for your third and, hopefully, final pit stop. In a full twenty-two seconds, you are fueled, have new right rubber, and are rolling back onto the track.

Three laps later the second-place car does not fare so well. Coming into the pits overly fast, the driver has to stand on the brakes, meanwhile killing his engine. By the time the crew has him restarted, thirty-six seconds have gone by.

The delay moves you into second place. But in your mirror you can see that you are being crowded by a charging Eagle-Offy and a Coyote-Ford, running third and fourth.

So you let everything out. Yet you are careful not to throw caution to the wind. You realize that a person can run 199 nearly perfect laps, then with a slight error lose the whole thing.

You keep creeping up behind the leader, knowing he sees you and hoping the sight will rattle him a little. But it doesn't, and he clings tenaciously to his narrowing lead through the 195th and 196th laps. Still, you are charging hard, and when he brakes a bit too much going into Turn 4, his machine wobbles uncertainly for a split second.

Since races are won or lost in just such split seconds, you dive low, hoping to take him on the inside. For one tottering instant you are sure that your wheels will lock. Then you are past!

From that moment on the race is all yours. Two laps later the white flag flashes before your eyes—one lap to go. But you hardly notice it. That last two and one-half miles can stretch into eternity, and you are holding a slippery lead. The close-up image of the second-place car jiggles in your mirror. So you hold down the throttle and flash in under the checkered flag going full out.

You take an extra insurance lap, hearing the roar of the crowd. Then you coast into the pit.

The aftermath gets a little confusing. Pummeled, blinded by cameras flashing, you are pushed to Victory Lane. You find yourself saying thank-you into microphones. A cork pops. You kiss the race queen, or vice versa. Someone helps you hold up the heavy trophy as more cameras flash.

Most of the celebration remains confusion, but you can sift it out later on. Right now happiness and the sheer exhilaration of victory are enough.

A formula sports racer gets the checkered flag.

GLOSSARY

Bent eight—V8 engine.
Big cubes—powerful engine with lots of cubic inches.
Binders—brakes.
Corner—a curve, or turn; or, as a verb, to maneuver through a curve.
Dicing—wheel-to-wheel racing.
Drafting—being pulled in the vacuum of the car ahead.
Esses—snakelike S-curves.
Formula—set of specifications covering car, motor, and the race itself.
Groove—best and shortest line around a race course.
Hang it on the wall—crash into a fence or barrier.
Hot iron—fast car.
Indy cars—big, open-cockpit, open-wheel championship cars.
Lose it—lose control of car and spin out.
Modified—a greatly altered racing car.
Monocoque—stress-formed, single-unit car body having no chassis framework as such.
Muscle car—a super-powered stock racer.
Production car—a car that is essentially as it comes off the salesroom floor, with power added.
Rubber—tires.
Stocker—ordinary car with added power.
Stroke it—drive no faster than necessary.
Wrench—a mechanic.

INDEX

indicates illustration

Accident, 83*, 86-88*, 90
American Road Race of Champions, 20
Automobile Competition Committee of the United States (ACCUS), 14
"Big Bangers," 33
Brakes (binders), 41, 82, 88-89
California 500, 15
Canadian-American Challenge Cup (Can-Am), 20-21
Cars
  balance of, 24-25; foreign, 11*, 36*; Grand Prix, 12-13; Group 7 Can-Am, 21*, 39*; midget, 15-16*, 24; pony, 22; small, 37*; special, 15; sports, 11, 16, 35-41, 37*, 38*, 39*, 65*; sprint, 15-16, 24
Centrifugal force, 24, 89
Championship car, 2*, 3*, 5*, 12, 15, 17*, 24-30*, 25*, 26*, 27*, 28*, 35, 56*, 66*, 73, 65*, 78*, 85*
Championship points, 22
Class, 21-22
Cockpit, 24, 27*, 74
Continental Championship, 21, 23
Chute (straight), 49, 89
Course (road), 45*
Corner (curve), 49

Daytona International Speedway, 20, 47*
"Dicing," 90, 91*
"Drafting," 89
Drag race strip, 53
Driver, 56*; licenses, 62; novice, 60-61; qualifications, 62; qualities, 55-57; training, 57-63
Engine, 22, 25, 28*-29, 34, 58-59, 67*, 76-77
Face shield, 70
Federation International de l'Automobile (FIA), 10, 14, 23, 62
Fire suit, 56*, 58*, 70, 75*
Flags, racing, 7, 61*-62, 78, 86, 90, 92-93*
Formula cars, 23, 28-30, 58*, 93*
Fuel, 26-27, 29, 33-35, 82*; cell, 69*; tank, 32
Fuelers, 83*, 85
Garage, 51, 64-65
Gasoline Alley, 26*, 51
Gloves, 58*, 63*, 75*
Grand American Challenge, 17-18
Grand Prix courses, 21, 23, 44-46
Groove, 7*, 59-60, 79, 86
Ground wire, 81-83

95

Helmet, 56*, 63*, 70, 75*
Horsepower, 21, 25, 27
Indianapolis Motor Speedway (Indy), 12*, 15, 20, 24-26*, 28, 43*, 53, 78*
Johnson Rod (scapegoat), 70
Laps, 77-79, 86
Lap money, 90-91
Mechanic (wrench), 2*, 3*, 50*, 64-72, 67*, 71*; chief, 66-70, 76; specialists, 67-68
Michigan International Speedway, 48
"Modifieds," 33-34
Monocoque, 40
National Association of Stock Car Racing (NASCAR), 16-18, 30-31, 62
National Championship, 12, 15
Ontario Motor Speedway (OMS), 24, 48-54*, 49*, 51*
Pace car, 74, 77
Padding, 24
Passing, 89-90
Pit, 50*, 71*, 81*, 83*; board, 72, 79, 80*; crew, 5*, 50*, 66-72, 76, 79-86, 81*, 82*, 85*; stop, 79-86, 81*, 82*, 85*
Points, 22
Pocono 500, 15, 24
Position, 78-79
Qualifying runs, 73
Race, 8*, 65*, 73-93, 74*, 75*, 76*, 78*, 80*, 81*, 82*, 83*, 85*, 87*, 88*, 91*, 93*;
direction, 24; history, 7-17; planning, 59-60; regulations, 10; track, 6*, 7*, 42-44, 53-54; types, 9
Road course, 42, 44-48, 53-54
Roll cage, 32
Safety, 32-34, 46, 54*, 69-70, 75, 83*, 84
Scoring, 52-53, 72
Speed, 17, 21, 26, 31, 86
Sports Car Club of America (SCCA), 18-21
Starter, 75-76*
Starting position, 73-74, 77
Steering wheel, 27*, 75
Stock car, 8*, 13*-14, 16-18*, 30-35, 32*, 33*, 45*, 47*, 71*
Straight, 49, 59, 78
Super speedway oval, 47*-54
Surface, 42-44, 50
Texas International Speedway, 48
Tires (rubber), 28-29, 31, 40*, 41, 58, 69, 80-84, 89
Trans-American Championship (Trans-Am), 20, 22
Trioval, 47-48
Triumph, 36*
United States Auto Club (USAC), 15-16, 62
Victory, 50, 93*
Weigh-in, 74*
Wheel, balance, 68*; suspension, 25, 28
World's Driver Champion, 23

96